Vernon Scannell, born in 1922, served with the Gordon
Highlanders in the Middle East and in the D–Day landings in
Normandy (see his autobiographical *Argument of Kings*). In his youth
he boxed both as amateur and professional and subsequently taught
English in a prep school but has been a full-time writer since the
early 1960s, publishing novels, criticism and four autobiographical
prose books as well as over a dozen volumes of poetry. An early
collection, *The Masks of Love* (1960) won the Heinemann Award,
The Loving Game (1975) was a Poetry Book Society Choice and he
has been awarded the Cholmondeley Poetry Prize and a Society of
Authors Travelling Scholarship. In 1980 he was granted a Civil List
Pension for services to Literature and he is an Honorary Fellow of
The Royal Society of Literature.

VERNON SCANNELL

Views and Distances

London
ENITHARMON PRESS
2000

First published in 2000
by the Enitharmon Press
36 St George's Avenue
London N7 0HD

Distributed in Europe
by Littlehampton Book Services
through Signature Book Representation
2 Little Peter Street
Manchester M15 4PS

Distributed in the USA and Canada
by Dufour Editions Inc.
PO Box 7, Chester Springs
PA 19425, USA

ISBN 1 900564 25 4

British Library Cataloguing-in-Publication Data.
A catalogue record for this book is available
from the British Library.

Set in 10.5pt Bembo by Bryan Williamson, Frome,
and printed in Great Britain by
The Cromwell Press, Wiltshire

CONTENTS

To John Coggrave

ACKNOWLEDGEMENTS

Acknowledgements are due to the editors of the following publica-
tions: *Ambit, The Critical Quarterly, The Formalist (USA), The
Interpreter's House, London Magazine, Orbis, Poetry Review, PN Review,
Poetry Wales, Rialto, Smith's Knoll, Stand, Times Literary Supplement*
and to the BBC World Service.

making comments about the world he sees. He real and mild
sometimes comic, sometimes compassionate but sharing with us
his views - making us look at things slightly differently. -
use of words particularly. cf. harsher & more biting Alan Bennett.
Northern touches.

UNRELIABLE ASSUMPTIONS

Hand-in-hand, smiling as they stroll,
The elderly man and woman pause to nod
Back at the municipal geraniums
Before resuming their unhurried trail
Towards the café near the swings and slide.

It would be easy to assume that this
Old couple had witnessed the dear, swift flight
Of fifty years or more of matrimony.
Not so. They met a month ago, or less,
At the *Darby and Joan* in Mercury Street.

It is unwise to make assumptions from
Observed appearances and signs. The roar
Of honking laughter from the Red Lion snug
Might mask distress, could even hide the dumb
Misery of absolute despair.

When my old friend, George Carmody, was seen
Leaving All Hallows after matins that Sunday,
And yet again at evensong, one might
Guess that he, improbably, had been
Converted, late, to Christianity.

But no, as Carmody himself confessed,
He had followed down the street a girl in frail
And flowery dress, sweet brevity of which
Revealed the longest, loveliest bare legs
That ever made eyes pop and breathing stall.

Those sleek and beckoning limbs had led him there
To lurk in musty shadows near the font
And watch the holy shaft of sunlight coax
Her hair to fine-spun gold, while bluish air
Was stained with rose-breath, wax, psalms' bready scent.

For most of that long summer Carmody
Was seen on Sunday in the sacred house.
Though there for heathen reasons, might not he
Have found in sermon, hymn and litany
At least a rumour of God's love and peace?

Well, no. Each Sunday, breathing pious air,
He had never felt more hopelessly alone,
And gazing at her aureate head would groan
Beneath the heavy sadness of desire,
Learn nothing that he had not always known.

BILLETS AIGRES

Early autumn, the first week
of October and a new love,
as leaves were turning in the watered milk
of morning mist they heard the click
in the hall and the sound of the fall,
not of sere leaves but the morning mail,
and with it a postcard, the first
of what would become a flood,
each picked for its power to shock, stop breath:
images of terror, torture, death.

At first by serious artists – Dürer,
Bosch and Munch – then came cruder cards,
each more violent and obscene,
and on the backs of all were scrawled
in a spiky hand he recognised
variations on one bleak theme,
short and soundless yelps of rage
and hatred. Every weekday morning
for more than eighteen months one dropped
from the letter-box. And then they stopped.

First they felt tentative relief and doubt;
then the sweet detoxifying silence grew,
and they began almost to forget
those daily shafts of hatred and the threats,
forgetting, too, the woman who
had uttered them, till one evening as he sat,
peaceful with Donne's poems on his lap,
a card fluttered down like a leaf from the sky –
a calm Corot landscape – and on the yellowing back
in that same spiky scrawl: 'I shall love you dear heart
till I die'.

THE GHOSTS OF LOVE

In the calm darkness of the moonless nights
those almost silent whisperings are heard:
the ghosts of love perform their timeless rites.

Not lovers' ghosts but shades of love's delights
return to haunt, with sigh or murmured word,
in the calm darkness of the moonless nights.

A disembodied voice of air recites
its litany of loss and, disinterred,
the ghosts of love perform their timeless rites.

The icy call of owl and star invites
the jilted lover to make up a third
in the calm darkness of the moonless nights.

Each place where passion flowered and rose in flights
of petals will remember this occurred:
the ghosts of love perform their timeless rites.

Though carnal vases may be smashed, their plight
beyond all aid, pathetic or absurd,
in the calm darkness of the moonless nights
the ghosts of love perform their timeless rites.

THE LONG HONEYMOON

They had been warned by the grey sages,
through homily or hint; not only though
by these, but others, too,
through word of mouth or print –
agony aunts and jaundiced divorcees –
that sexual passion could not ever last.

But they ignored all warnings
and advice; they settled down together
to discover, after ten years,
the sweet and heady spice
of carnal love no less delicious, even
tastier than it had been in the past.

Only last night they each
explored the other as if they'd never known
those parts before, writhing
in warm conjunction, rolling over,
recumbent dance, the bed their ballroom floor;
and then they slept, in stillness, like the dead.

Yet dawn saw them awake
to dance again, tempo more andante,
twirls less wild, but never
a touch of weariness or strain.
Next evening, when he whispered, 'Bed?' she smiled.
'I think I'm just a bit too tired,' she said.

CHANGING ROLES

Where are those lovely girls we used to know,
The dreamy Juliets and cool Cordelias,
Vivacious Rosalinds and pale Ophelias,
Tall tigerish Helens, the dark or golden flow
Of all that lustrous, lilac-scented hair
Now all of them have taken different parts?
Where are those smiles that pierced our panting hearts,
The creamy robes of flesh they used to wear?

They've put on wiry wigs and wrinkled masks;
They move arthritically and sing like crows.
I wonder though if any of them asks,
'Whatever happened to those Romeos?'

A few might just be trusted with a spear,
But most look like that mad old fool King Lear.

THE EMPEROR'S DAUGHTER

Exquisite and bare
beneath the silken duvet
no lover may share

she smiles, nearing sleep,
and counts her hapless suitors
trailing past, like sheep.

LES BELLES DAMES

Reflected in the troubled looking-glass
of tall shop-windows' tilted, smooth lagoons,
not plain enough for you to make a guess
at colour of the eyes, or even hair –
except that you would know it dark or fair –
they haunt these late autumnal afternoons.

Their other, more substantial, avatars,
released from vitreous immurement, seem
even less attainable than those,
though no less lovely as their dainty feet
chatter like castanets along the street,
while they dance out of sight and into dream.

Their milieu is the City – Rome, New York,
Paris, the Smoke. They are not Zion's daughters,
with wanton eyes and undulating walk,
whose haunches mime the ocean's heaves and dips
and signal to the punters: *Read my hips* –
their message faintest music over waters.

There is, for thwarted seekers, only this
hope of something like a rendezvous,
which has to be in sleep's metropolis
where, white and slender in blue evening air,
as innocent as cigarettes once were,
they open wide their arms; then fade from view.

LOST PROPERTIES

These are not docketed and tidied away
in cabinets on main-line railway stations
but are scattered over tracts of time and place
to be revisited, perhaps, but never
reclaimed. Item: a pair of flimsy yellow
knickers seen on a Sunday morning, tangled
in brambles on the edge of Roundhay golf-course;
and, later the same day – or so it now seems –
close to the lake in the park, on unstartled
grass, a single red shoe with stiletto heel,
sad in its abandoned, tawdry elegance.

I do not think it likely that there could be
two different owners of these lost properties,
nor am I confident that I shall ever
see their bereft possessor, though a small wick
of hope is not quite extinguished. I return
quite often to these sedgeless, unchanged places,
and, though it may be revenant rather than
corporeal woman haunting the lakeside,
I feel one day she might appear, limping
on single red stiletto heel, the pale curve
of cold cheeks vulnerable in songless air.

DOCTORS

Doctors walk swiftly down corridors and wear
white coats with stethoscopes dangling either from
their pockets or worn like drab chains of office.
Men and women, they are all young, well under
forty, and all of them are very handsome.
When they smile, mischievous at the pretty nurse
or reassuringly at the aged patient,
it is with teeth perfectly white and even.

These are the doctors we see on our screens
and they do not much resemble the ones we meet
in shabby consulting-rooms whose smiles, if there,
are rather tired and probably display teeth
not quite the white of fresh aspirin as they
enquire about bowel-movement, waterworks
and known allergies to antibiotics
before tapping out nostrums on computers.

Other doctors exist or have existed
of course but these, too, aren't likely to be seen
in TV soaps wearing dangling stethoscopes,
for these are the Teachers, Doctors of Music,
Philosophy, Literature and Law, many
quite famous and revered though not for white smiles
or dark curly hair: Doctors Johnson and Donne
and the composer of *Rule Britannia*, Arne.

There are also Doctors of Divinity
and Doctors of the Church, Aquinas, Anselm,
Teresa of Avila, Francis of Sales,
to be revered though not carnally desired.
But when molested by pains and lack of breath
it is the unglamorous, overworked man
or woman we seek out, not the beautiful
or the holy who would frighten us to death.

ROUGH BOYS

was a common appellation in my childhood
for describing lads from families and districts
even poorer than our own. 'Rough' was relative
of course. To the elegant and perfumed mothers
of the blazered and well-shod boys from the houses
with gardens, whose dads worked in banks or offices,
my brother Ken and I would have been considered
unquestionably rough. No doubt Mrs Spender
would have been careful to keep little Stephen
safe from the risk of meeting one or both of us.

But there were rougher boys, by far, than Ken and me.
I'll name a few: Stink Holbrow, Doggie Percival,
Dump Rickard, Mockle Welch and Chinaman Cheney,
all of them addressed, as you see, by soubriquets.
We did not know their Christian names, each cognomen
as mysterious then as now, except for Stink,
whose pungent presence could have been detected in
blindfold darkness at a dozen paces or more.

Chinaman Cheney was killed at Narvik. Rickard
died early from strong drink, or so it was rumoured.
As for the others, I have lost all trace of them
but, whether living or dead, they have become ghosts,
still scowling their menace from corners in ginnels
or swearing and spitting on the truant towpath
of the Grand Union Canal, where they still wait
to ambush their victims, sissies with neat partings
and leather satchels holding virtuous homework,
the rough boys who don't grow old as we who are left
with our given names grow old or invisible;
and when, in the whispering classroom, the register
is called, all, present or absent, answer their names.

THE K.O. CULTURE

Differences were settled with a punch,
Though crack of fist on jaw would always seem
Too sharp, the sound of speeding billiard-balls
Colliding with abrupt and bony *clack*;
No real punch on the jaw could sound like that.
But these encounters happened on the screen,
And we believed, in some platonic sense,
That those right-hooks were real, not like our own
Wild swings in back street, bar or football-stand,
Which missed completely or smashed up your hand,
And hurt the striker far more than the struck.

Our heroes and exemplars might be tough
Stetsoned cowpokes wearing neckerchiefs,
Leathery chaps in leather chaps and spurs,
Whose fist-fights were conducted in the bars
Of honky-tonk saloons; or they could be
Gangsters in fedoras, just as quick
With uppercut or haymaker as gun.
But these were not the only ones who punched;
Even Catholic priests could use their mitts.
You hardly ever saw a film in which
No character got walloped on the chin.

Even debonair society dudes,
When cross, or crossed in love, knocked culprits cold.
Remember them? Tuxedoed, brilliantined,
The Roberts – Taylor, Young, Montgomery –
William Powell and Melvyn Douglas, all
Capable of flattening a cad
As coolly as they lit a cigarette
In frothy comedies. It's what they did,
And what we did as well, or not so well,
Or tried our best to do if we were mocked,
Insulted, wronged in any way. We socked.

And, as I've said, we often missed or bust
Our fist on ivory skull, or else we found
Ourselves entangled with the adversary,
Undignified and rolling on the ground.
Absurd. And yet one sometimes heaves a sigh
For those, the K.O. days, when we replied
To insult with a quick right-cross. Or tried.
Surely better than the baseball-bat,
Machete, knife or, worst of all, the gun
That now replace the fist, off-screen and on —
If things have ever truly been like that.

IN REGENT'S PARK

amusing & yet poignant

Above the tower-blocks' squinting geometries
A homing jet slides down the silky sky,
Its human freight invisible to us
As we to them with those things we can see,
Slow juggling of bright traffic lights, the heap
Of crumpled misery slumped upon the bench
Inside the park, whose mimicry of sleep
Permits no rest or respite from the stench
Of what he has become. No healing dreams
For him and yet, close by, in that same park,
The famous summer Dream unfolds and holds
Both players and an audience that seems
Entranced, although two folk from Portland, Maine,
Express vague puzzlement because, for them,
Ass and Bottom are straight synonyms.

DELIVERING THE GOODS

verbal dexterity

1

Good in Bed

An expression used more in literary
dialogue, perhaps, than in quotidian
exchanges among friends and acquaintances;
a term that is employed far more frequently
by women (both fictive and real) than by men,
usually referring to the other sex.
This, if true, may be because of the greater
spiritual generosity of women
who are more often ready to discover
some small saving virtue in the otherwise
entirely contemptible male.
                    We all know
what is meant of course, in a general way,
yet nevertheless this conjunction of words
transmits semantic discords: for example,
is the man or woman who is 'good in bed'
good only in bed? Does virtue leak away
when a vertical position is assumed?
Surely such moral exemplars as Mother
Teresa were as good in bed as they were
out of it.
                    Origen must have been as good
as it is possible to be, according
to his own beliefs, for Eusebius claimed
that this wise and virtuous philosopher
removed from his own body those instruments
which occasion sin; or, to put it plainer,
he cut his bollocks off.
                    But of course we know
that the 'good' in 'good in bed' does not imply
moral rectitude, but this is not to say
its opposite is necessarily there.
The 'good in bed' must be imaginative,
inventive, tender, grateful and unselfish,
qualities that even Origen would not

23

condemn when exercised in other places.
But, however passionate the players seem,
they will not be truly good unless each knows,
after the fierce fortissimo crescendo,
the sigh, in the dark, of love's unfolding rose.

ii

Good for Nothing

Good for nothing, a favourite phrase
My father used as he would glower,
Enraged by what I seemed to him to be;
Of course I knew, by his fierce gaze
And look of chewing something sour,
He did not mean to praise or flatter me.

The words themselves, though, puzzled me
Whichever way I looked at them,
For *good* and *nothing* didn't seem to mate,
Would always, surely, disagree
Like *precious fake* or *worthless gem*;
I couldn't see what they might designate.

Good was fine and positive
While *nothing* was – well, vacancy;
And I – the Old Man claimed – was good for this;
How I, or anyone, could give
Virtue to sheer nullity
Was quite beyond me then, and it still is.

He called my brother, Kenneth, *ape*
And rarely used his given name.
I was a *pup*. I think perhaps his head
Held beasts, whose one way of escape
Was through his mouth. Was he to blame?
Who knows, or cares, now that the bastard's dead.

Good Eggs

affirmation of the
power of love

From the fridge he carefully selects
two eggs and holds them both in the palm
of his left hand for her inspection.

They are smooth and brown. She nods assent,
then takes them from him and, with a pin,
deftly pricks the rounder end of each.

Next, she places both eggs in a bowl
of warm water, second stratagem
against their cracking. Her final trick

is to add a generous pinch of salt
to the bubbling water in the pan.
Then it is for him to take the eggs,

one at a time, in a table-spoon,
from the warm bowl and transfer them to
the boiling water. He checks the clock,

then watches as she lays out the plates,
spoons and cups while the eggs are nudging
each other in the steaming saucepan.

It is good again to watch her move
about the room, graceful though without
self-consciousness, and he is surprised

by a sudden pinprick of bright joy
that these shared simplicities should bring
a new-laid world, fresh every morning.

iv
Good Grief

It is not here among the fragrant rites,
The flowers and summer dresses in the cool
Twilight of the nave where slanting lights
From clerestory and gilded oriel fall,
Gleaming softly on the polished box
Which, to our puzzled eyes, seems far too small
To hold his broken body and which mocks
Our shattered notions of the brave and tall;
Nor can the muted music's wiliest arts –
His favourite Dvořák, Beethoven and Brahms –
Coax it to the chill vault of our hearts
Or hold us safe in reassuring arms.

Though those diminished sevenths seem to float
The scent of all June's flowers made audible,
And loop a noose of honey round the throat,
We find their blandishments implausible.
Some facile tears expressed, a sob or two,
But grief, true grief, is scentless, drab, elsewhere,
And that elsewhere, which waits for me and you
Beyond the cypress, marble crosses, square
White or lichened tablets of carved stone,
Is silent, cold, and it will not permit
Entry save to those who are alone;
And this is where we must contend with it,
The grief that does not heal or mitigate
The pain of loss, yet must be understood
As necessary and will predicate
Its cauterizing hurt as final good.

V

Good at English

humour.

He never was much good at school,
Couldn't bowl and couldn't bat;
On the football field a fool,
And in the classroom worse than that,
    Except, of course, at English.

Mathematics baffled him;
He had no memory for dates;
Latin made his poor head swim
But he could quote you scads of Yeats,
    For he was good at English.

Almost bottom of the form,
Main butt of masters' dusty wit
And bait for bullies in the dorm,
It did not seem to help a bit
    That he was good at English.

Nor did it help when, schooling done,
He sought employment which might bring
Wealth and status, even fun,
But found there was no opening
    For someone good at English.

At last he got a job and still
Works there, at the G.P.O.,
Selling stamps behind a grille
To people who will never know
    That he was good at English.

At home he keeps a family –
A wife who fades, two boys who grow –
And he and they would all agree
He's not much good at that, although
    He once was good at English.

Good Citizen

At the edge of the copse, nervous branches
squirm before his face.
He watches, does not move close.
The child's gold head pores over buttercups,
parasoling daisies. She is very beautiful.
The mother smiles dreamily in the sun.
When both have gone he shrugs the shadows off
and walks towards the town.

Next morning he catches his usual train.
Opposite are biteable thighs, smooth knees
like new potatoes. He raises his paper and reads
black commentaries. The air
quivers with lavender and musk.
The carriage sways and stumbles on the rails,
strains against thrust. He lowers his paper
and stares her boldly in the knees.

On Sunday morning the cat on his lawn
holds a bird in its mouth; the seeds of its eyes
are alive and bright. The cat is proud.
He eats roast lamb for lunch, then sleeps.
On his way to evensong he bows
to familiar faces on the street.
He is the good citizen, the friendly neighbour.

vii
Good Time

How that ravenous abstraction, Time,
can own the quality of goodness, goodness
knows; and yet we say it all the time.

Have a good time is simple, I suppose;
at least we catch the drift: enjoy yourself,
get drunk, get laid, get tanned, or all of those.

Joy buds and flowers in Time, that's understood;
that which is indispensable to bliss,
its soil and habitation, must be good.

But when they say, as they quite often do,
all in good time, what can be meant by this?
I've used the phrase myself, and so have you.

No one, though, has ever told us why
the time is 'good' that everything is in:
I can't explain, however hard I try.

Language games are always hit or miss;
you might not learn much but they can be fun.
In fact I had a good time writing this.

HEARING AID

'Leopards pray,'
the surpliced voice intoned
from the Sunday morning radio.

The listener saw the furry creatures,
paws together, eyes half-closed,
a scene that William Blake might have composed.

On 'The World at One'
a different voice spoke of the need
for screaming pregnant women,

and the same listener saw
shrill images from Bosch or Fuseli
of female suffering and man's indifference.

Later in the day, on Radio 4,
a play was trailed: *Goats*, by Henry Gibson;
a bucolic comedy, no doubt.

And then the listener's wife
said, 'I've found it. Here. You left it in the loo,
as you so often do.'

Evening: Radio 3.
'The Great C Major', words now clear,
the image vivid, too:

Tall, muscular and lean
in full dress uniform,
a stern, bemedalled Royal Marine.

YORKSHIRE DANDY

On Friday night you might observe him,
    a man of uncertain years
dressed in reactionary clothing
    who nevertheless appears
to display a certain stylish elegance
    that you do not often see
at any time in the centre of
    Otley and most certainly
not at 10pm in Boroughgate
    where already evidence
of an over-indulged appetite
    for a superabundance
of Tetley's bitter and fish and chips
    may be detected upon
the pavement where he carefully steps
    as he, too, is eating from –
not polystyrene or *The Bradford*
    Telegraph and Argus – but
The Times Literary Supplement
    and his hot supper is not
fishcake, cod, haddock, or even plaice,
    but sole meunière with what
else but *frites* and his belly contains
    a chilled Chardonnay and not
ten pints of Tetley's or John Smith's,
    nor does he bellow randy
needs to deaf skies or, alfresco, piss,
    for he is the Yorkshire Dandy.

AL BOWLLY ON THE COSTA DEL SOL

Afternoon in February.
Back in England poor sods shiver,
or so we meanly hope.
Here, in Andalucia, tingling sunshine
ices walls and terraces
and turns the iron grills
to fancy liquorice sticks.
We sit in our white room, the window wide,
eating bread and olives,
drinking *vino tinto*
while the radio plays
songs from those camphor-scented days
between the two Great Wars.

The tempo sets
bunioned feet tap-tapping to the beat
and, somewhere else,
yet also somehow here,
the dancers take the floor.
The men's strong arms
lightly hold the sweet and lovely girls
with something in their eyes,
not quite angelic now
that angels are so few
but, while at least the songs are sung,
they'll string along with you.

So close your eyes
and rest your head
here on my shoulder while,
in the haunted ballroom, tall
and handsome dancers in white ties and tails
take partners for the last waltz and begin
their graceful circumambulations till
the saxophones have melted to a slur
of liquid silver on the midnight floor
and all the dancers turn and turn,
like those old HMVs
which, once they'd sung their song,
slowed down and down and then, at last, were still.

DRINK PROBLEM

You should not trust the testimony of drunks,
They romanticise what is, at best,
a risky pleasure and, at worst,
a dark seductress who will kill when minded to.
But look – I, too, have started on the game
of making metaphors, mythologising
in the usual woolly way
of shabby poets with red eyes and noses
and hands that shake. It will not do. Dismiss
those tales of noble topers, the eloquent and wild,
bardic boozers, holy fools, the brilliant and the doomed.
Recognise the drab or foul realities:
vomit, shame, remorse, the fractured mind
and furred intelligence, the taste of knives,
and, always there, the metaphysical stink
that drenches you and can't be washed away.
This is the drunkard's lot; the briefest glance –
like this one now,
side-long, shifty, quick to slither off –
is quite enough to drive a wagon-load
of sober prosemen straight on to the booze.

NEGATIVE REFLECTIONS ON AQUINAS

I have managed to resist, without too much distress,
The temptation to read *Summa Contra Gentiles*,
And my favourite bedside reading has never been
Summa Theologica. I recall having seen,
Or heard, that Saint Thomas Aquinas somewhere claims
That the Saved in Heaven can look down at the flames
Of Hell through a handy peep-hole in Paradise,
Savouring the torments of the Damned by this device.

Proclaimed Doctor of the Church in 1567,
Aquinas promised that we could get to Heaven
If we followed this piece of advice: 'Live each day
As if it were your last.' There must be another way.

Your last? Live every single day of your life in stark
And gibbering terror of the coming dark? No way.

CLOSE SHAVE

Morning clangs outside in North Street, Otley.
On with – once again – the shabby motley.
Before that, though, a piss and then a shave;
And so it goes, and will go, to the grave.

You start the tedious ritual once more
And smear your chops, as you have done before
A thousand times, with Father Christmas stuff;
And then you scrape away the feathery fluff.

One little nick. Not bad. It's time to rinse
And dry your face, splash aftershave and wince
At styptic on the cut. The sting soon goes;
Ahead, the day's grey page of turbid prose.

How many more small cuts and shaves remain?
You'd rather not be told. But this is plain:
That's one less scrape-and-lather to be done.
And is this any consolation? None.

ANOTHER VIEW OF THANATOS

Death be not proud! Why not? You've got good cause.
Mighty and dreadful? Yes, we're bound to call
You both of these since you have fathered all
Our best achievements, art and healing, laws,
Rituals to ease the pain that gnaws
On hearts and minds till desperations scrawl
Their shrill graffiti on the falling wall:
You justly claim respect, if not applause

But few of us will tender thanks though you
Persuade us to erect great domes of thought
And pallisades of piety to thwart
Your fruitful menaces. Yet this is true:
You frighten me to death old sport;
If I had half your power, then I'd swank too.

IN THE CHAIR

Steel bangles clamp wrists;
head is half-nelsoned by a rigid arm,
feet fastened firm.

Buttocks are clenched like fists;
I am not comfortable
but do not complain.

I would be content to sit here
for a very long time,
forever if I could.

But I know, almost,
that in seconds I must go.
The bald walls blur,

voices in the gallery
melt to a running slur.
Soon I shall be a nasty memory.

Blind, between my thighs,
my sex is shrivelled to a dead wince,
could cause now little offence

as out of sight, anonymous,
the clean hand reaches for the switch
to grasp and throw it down.

I will sit this dance out
as the lights in the cell-blocks dim
and the orchestra of mugs and spoons begins.

AUBADE

'Rain before dawn,'
is what the weather-forecaster had said,
and he was right.
I heard it niggling at the window-pane
when I awoke,
uneasy in the deep, unsleeping night.

It was also
sweeping, with soft and patient industry,
pavements and roads,
gleaming feebly in the dark below.
The world might be
a little cleaner when the sun arose.

When the first, faint
intimation of almost light slid
a slender strip
of steeliness between thin curtain-gap
I heard a sound
quite different from the rainfall's hiss and tap.

It was the drum
of marching feet approaching close, and then
abrupt full-stop
of studs. A yelped command to load, then slam
of rifle-bolts.
It could have been a dream, but it was not.

'Hi! What you got in that blue file?'

'My essay for old Zimmermann.
   I should a finished it last week
but I kept stalling. Then I ran
clean out of all excuses, so
Stayed up all night to finish it.
That's why I'm feeling knackered now.'

'Yeah, I thought you looked like shit.
What's your essay all about?'

'Hopkins's Terrible Sonnets.'

                                     Who
was Hopkins then?'

                          'Oh, some old priest,
a Jesuit.'

                          'And was it true?'

'What true?'

                          'His sonnets, were they all
really terrible? If so
how come he got to publish them?'

'Yeah, pretty awful. I don't know.'

SMALL EXPECTATIONS

The promised pleasure comes at last, then goes
So swiftly, leaving little after-taste.
Is this the most we can expect? God knows.

In summer's drought we long for winter snows.
They fall and melt away to leave bleak waste;
The promised pleasure comes at last, then goes.

The steely river melts and water flows.
Spring's brief refurbishment is soon defaced.
Is this the most we can expect? God knows.

At last the ardent lover holds the rose
Of long desire, that creaminess unlaced.
The promised pleasure comes at last, then goes.

And is there nothing more she can disclose?
Must every gem reveal itself as paste?
Is this the most we can expect? God knows.

Not all caresses surely, turn to blows,
Nor every dainty maiden prove unchaste?
The promised pleasure comes at last, then goes.
Is this the most we can expect? God knows.

When Uncle Walter died he left behind
A heap of clothes, all of them consigned
To me, drab legacy. Walter had been
A man of substance, physically I mean,
Well over six feet tall and hefty, too.
So, of those suits and jackets, very few
If any would be worn by me, although
Among the camphor-scented pile I spied
One garment that I just might wear outside
The privacy of home. I pulled it out,
An overcoat of heavy stuff, about
Half a century old, but still quite smart,
Expensive triumph of the cutter's art.

This was the winter of 1963
And though the coat was far too big for me
The vicious icy weather swept away
What doubts I might have felt. So I went swathed
From chin to ankles, hem an inch or so
Above the ground and trailing in the snow.

The first time that it went on public show
Was in 'The George' saloon, Great Portland Street
Where BBC producers used to meet
With actors, poets, lovers, friends and foes.
I felt uneasy, knowing some of those
Work and pleasure rivals would be quick
To exercise their wit and rhetoric
If my enormous overcoat seemed weird,
As I thought likely. I need not have feared.

Three people spoke of it, and all expressed
Surprise at seeing me so swishly dressed.
One, a younger man than I, a Beat
Poet from the wilds of Charlotte Street,
Begged with passion to discover where
I'd found it and he offered then and there
To buy it, throwing in his own coat free.
I was in step with fashion then. I see
In this small tale a little allegory,
A kind of metaphor for things apart
From those sartorial: for poetry, for art.

The old coat was discarded years ago.
My clothes are out of fashion now, although
I sometimes think that, if I keep them so,
Perhaps the time will come around when they
Again seem up to date. But I must say
This seems unlikely. Could anyone suppose
A craze for doublet and cross-gartered hose?
Impossible. But then, one never knows.

POETIC ENCOUNTERS

The first poem to thrill and resound
in his skull and finger his senses,
awakening, too, a curious
and pleasurable sadness,
was called 'He Fell Among Thieves'.
Its author was Sir Henry Newbolt.

Odd that a ten-year-old boy, living
in a bleak street of squinting dwellings
with shit-houses in the small back-yards,
should have been moved and haunted
by images of School Close
and Chapel, morning rides with father.

Not so odd that the second poem
to beguile him was Masefield's 'Cargoes',
that dance of rich flavours and colours,
tang and tingle of contrast.
For years he thought 'quinquereme'
was the name of an exotic fruit.

Now, knowing differently does not rob
the quinquereme of juice and fragrance
but increases the heft of the word;
and that yearning memory
of the never-known good place
still stirs in the wake of the poem.

POET TREE

Until he reached the age of nine or ten
He lived in places north of Birmingham,
At first in Beeston, Nottinghamshire, and then
In Eccles, Lancashire, where he began
At school to learn by heart the wizard words
That, he was told, were known as 'poitry',
Words that soared and swooped and sang like birds,
Or rumbled in the dark mysteriously.

The vowel in 'poitry' rhymed, of course, with 'boy'.
Next, the family moved south, a place
Not far from London where they might enjoy
A better life – though this proved not the case –
And here at school he heard an alien sound:
The teacher spoke of 'poetry', the first
Syllable rhymed with cockney 'dough'. He found
His mind befogged, but then the mist dispersed.

Suddenly he saw the marvellous thing
Quite plain in silvery sunlight, tall, serene
Against blue sky, its branches blossoming
In multicoloured vocables from green
Syllabic buds, the flowering Poet Tree,
Where for centuries fabled birds had sung,
And under whose protecting canopy
Poets had dreamed, or from its branches swung.

A BINYON OPINION

They went with songs to the battle, they were young,
Straight of limb, true of eye, steady and aglow.
They were staunch to the end against odds uncounted,
They fell with their faces to the foe.

They shall grow not old, as we that are left grow old: . . .
Laurence Binyon, 'For The Fallen'

I was there, at Wipers and the Somme.
I left one leg at some place near Cambrai
And counted myself lucky, not like Tom,
My pal, what I won't see till Judgement Day.

So when this civvy poet says they 'fell
With faces to the foe' it don't sound right.
My pal, he never fell. A Jerry shell
Smashed him up to smithereens that night.

Another thing he says that's far from true:
That they — and he means us — was 'straight of limb'.
But half of our platoon, I swear to you,
Had bandy legs and wasn't tall and slim.

He says — and he means Tom and all those poor
Lads that got wiped out — 'they won't grow old',
As if it's something to be thankful for.
They aint no Peter Pans. They're muck and mould.

They're dead, and Death's 'august and royal'
This poet claims. In civvy street maybe
It looks like that. These fibs make my blood boil.
Tom's dead and I'm alive — well, most of me.

46

NOVEMBER 11th 1997

Again the grey survivors try to call
Back from the dark the dead who now have lain
Too long in heedless dust to entertain
Much hope of resurrection in this Fall.
The damp and jaundiced leaves will soften all
The studded noise of marching feet. The stain
Of crimson on the gauze of mist and rain
Will never lure them from their vaulted hall.

I see two friends as they were long ago,
Images the heaped years can't displace,
Bill Gray whose guts were splattered in the snow,
Jim Rennie, picked off by a sniper's shot.
At least they have escaped what we now face:
You'd think this might console, but it does not.

WORD GAMES

Rhyme and readers

Things we utter without thinking,
as we chatter while we're drinking
or companionably strolling
through the meadows and the rolling
hills of favourite country walks,
sometimes, or you might say fairly
often, carry meanings rarely
thought of by the casual speaker,
meanings odder, maybe bleaker,
than belong in easy talks.

Phrases such as 'hit or miss'
could mean 'musical success
or unmarried lady'. Also
'hit' could signify a blow
with wielded weapon or a punch,
and 'miss' mean when the knuckly bunch
fails to find the aimed-at nose.

Depending largely on the context,
elementary terms have quite vexed
listeners with receivers tuned to
other stations: 'bats and balls' you
might think unambiguous,
but 'bats' could be small belfry-haunters
linked, improbably, with dancers –
a bit far-fetched, it's true.

'Pros and cons' would make most Majors
think at once of golf-instructors
in the company of jailbirds,
while other-ranks could see some ladies
of the night involved in scams.

Bookish people might have reason
hearing that well-known expression
'nick of time', to think of Auden's
'prison of his days' where free men
are instructed 'how to praise'.

But enough of double meanings
though, for all of you with leanings
to the lexically ludic,
I'll leave, to see how you might view it,
'tit for tat', a common phrase,
like to provoke a titter,
though not perhaps among the liter-
ati, those whose brows might rise
just a little higher than ever.
So now I'll leave these words for you:
'tit for tat', and toodle-oo.

LOSING WEIGHT

It is something you have long desired.
Tired of lugging your load of fat
that blankets bone, tired of going slow,
you yearn to wear leanness, ache to amaze
your friends, enrage fat foes and plump wife:
life would be a lot better like that,
batter-pudding belly gone for good,
handsome, muscular, sleek as a cat.
But wait! This must be understood:

you can't expect your pectorals to swell
a steel cuirass, nor stomach ape
washboard corrugations, biceps and triceps
ripple and bulge, weight-lifter's thighs,
the waist of a supple dancer of tangoes;
too late, alas, by far, for those.

Maybe better, after all, to walk
stout and slowly on the shorter route,
unseductive and resigned
to being outpaced and scorned by the slender,
but not yet in immediate danger
of stripping down to the moon-white bone
the undiscriminating denizens of earth
will welcome to their dark, well-furnished home.

PREMATURE EJACULATIONS

'Oh, goodness me!' he cried, and, 'Oh my word!'
Though nothing whatsoever had occurred.

MUMMY

You stand at the window, mummy,
In the picture I have of you
With your permanent wave and your cupid's bow lips
And frock with waistline hugging your hips
And your eyes of such deep-sea blue.

No wonder the whole world loved you
And the beaux lined up to woo.
You looked like a movie star,
I'd have paid for a seat to watch you eat
The hearts they served up for you.

But what was it made you choose
The man with the Aryan nose
And big black coat and a hook of steel
Instead of a hand, and an iron mouth
That chomped and swallowed you?

But I could make him spew.
He just had to look at me,
And that's what he did, he up-threw,
And you were as good as new,
Once I'd mopped all the goo off of you.

Mummy, you're looking good now,
All I want is you.
We've got rid of the shit in the bottomless pit
And now it's just me and you.
Mummy, mummy, you darling, it's true.

BOOK OF DAYS

At first, each day is blank, anonymous,
until you write or print or paint on it:
an empty page, of course quite meaningless.

Before you see the baker's shop is shut,
and hear church-bells and sniff the sizzling roast,
you wouldn't know which day you're looking at.

The click and whisper of the morning post,
or telephone's soft rasp, might start a new
twist in story-line and change the gist

of yesterday's account, then lead you to
territory you've never seen before,
that might, or might not, please and welcome you.

No one really knows what lies in store,
whatever calendars and stars may say;
but, if you hear a knocking at the door,

and irritably bawl out, 'Go away!'
it's yours to choose: your caller might have been
a long-limbed lovely who had come to stay,

or pale Jehovah's Witness with a clean-
cut countenance and drab but well-pressed suit,
or someone out of nightmare with a gun.

The girl, though, might have picked up some acute
sexually-transmitted sickness, while
the bible-tout could be the one who'd shoot.

You never know your luck. You might compile
a great thick wad of days, or you might not;
either way they'll tell a kind of tale

though, long or short, it won't contain a plot;
no dénouement, of course, where there's no knot.

CONTENT AND DISCONTENT

I sit at the kitchen table, lunch finished;
rain whispers at the window; pale asterisks
splash against the pane, then vanish.

Pascal Rogé, on the 'wireless' as I still call it,
performs Ravel's *Concerto for Piano Left Hand*:
bright notes swarm from his clever mitt.

This work was commissioned by Paul Wittgenstein,
who gave his good right arm for the Fatherland,
a brave as well as a gifted man.

Open, on the table next to my side-plate,
is Frances Partridge's *A Pacifist's War*,
diaries kept during the second Big Fight

against the Germans from 1939
to '45, and on the plate can be seen
what is left of a Spice Pippin core.

It is many months since I wrote a poem.
Once, I might have been moved to write about
Wittgenstein's laying down of one arm

and his subsequent defiance and glory;
or something on music and the Second World War,
or even choose to celebrate once more

the taste and shape and mythopoeic power
of apples, their beauty and sheer appleness;
but I've tried all these before.

Music and apples, love, sacrifice and war –
all done with. It seems that I have quite run out
of things to write about;

except, maybe, this bankruptcy could offer
something in the way of subject-matter.
And it does: not much, though, to write home about.

VIEWS AND DISTANCES

They sit together on their stolen towel
and count their few remaining francs and days
of dear vacation. Out in the bay the sea,
a crinkled spread of shimmering blue, sustains
an elegant white yacht at anchor there,
and, as they gaze, they see that, on the deck,
a man and woman have appeared who lean
languid at the vessel's rail and seem,
improbably, to offer stare for stare.

At night the sky's dark blue is deeper still,
is almost black. The rigging of the yacht
is hung with fairy-lights, and music drifts
and scents the air. The man in his white tux
and woman in her Dior gown still seem
to peer towards the shore as if they might
see once more the morning's teasing sight –
the enviable simplicities of youth
and deprivation, envy, appetite.

SOME TIMES

'Time will tell,' said his grannie,
So he asked her what it would say;
But all she would tell him was: 'Quite a lot,
As you will find out one day.'

'Time flies,' his mother murmured.
'Where does it fly to?' he said.
'Over the mountains and over the seas.
Now off you go to bed.'

'I'm beating time,' said his father,
As he tapped his foot in the sun.
But the music stopped, and the band went home,
And time it was that won.

SILENCE

Defined as absence of all sound, and yet
a presence, ubiquitous and positive,
a necessary palimpsest to give
white space for various musics to be set
with words and other signs – the cryptic fret
of abstract traceries in time, a sieve
in which we separate the sparkling, live
birdsong from the glinting barrel's threat.

It is never absolute, not while the heart's
diastole and systole persist,
and human expirations mime the arts
of zephyrs waking leaves' green speech, and mist
the glass that shows who stays and who departs;
not while the pulse beats in the tender wrist.

DEAD STARS

Last night I thought again of all the stars —
I don't mean those that prink the midnight sky,
which clever guys with telescopes can parse
and analyse and coolly classify —
not Sirius, the brightest of them all,
red giant or white dwarf, nor heads of pins
that pricked romantic skies we all recall
from tales in which the young prince always wins.

No, I thought of Gable, Stewart, Flynn,
Bogart, Tracy, Cooper and John Wayne;
thought, also, of those heavenly bodies in
their skin-tight velvet, Crawford and Fontaine,
Dietrich, Ava Gardner, Alice Faye,
still glowing in the dark, light years away.

SESTINA OF SUNDAY MUSIC

Another Sunday evening; darkness falls
earlier now each day and I have drawn
the curtains long ago. Faint, distant calls
of nameless creatures pencil their forlorn
needs on silence's soft slate. Dry leaves
outside converse in whispers. A thin wind grieves.

Inside, a different kind of music grieves:
a measured threnody unfolds and falls
in melting pearls that form a pool which leaves
rich sonic fragrance in the air. Then, drawn
from woodwinds' lamentations and forlorn
complaints of strings, float wraiths of bugle-calls.

This is the Sunday music that recalls
dim images of loss and one who grieves
and gazes over moorland more forlorn
than twilit fields of crosses. Here rain falls
unceasingly. Gun-carriages, horse-drawn,
move with small thunder muffled by moist leaves.

It is not only genius that leaves
its legacy of melody which calls
our hearts to mastering heel where they are drawn
to passionate compliance: Rudolfo grieves
as poignantly as Dido. Waterfalls
of richness drench, but leave us still forlorn.

Whoever writes the score, the same forlorn
message is received. The years, like leaves,
are heaped beneath the trees; the last one falls,
and then the man in sable clothing calls.
Love can't be weighed by how the widow grieves.
Like all the hard-fought contests this is drawn.

Violins are beautiful as objects drawn
by master draughtsmen; even the forlorn
stone-or-tone-deaf solitary who grieves
apart perceives the sweep of sound that leaves
shapes of unuttered song, and so he calls
'Encore!' before the final curtain falls.

Then he, too, falls. The orchestra's withdrawn
and no more curtain-calls; the drained, forlorn
audience leaves, and darkening silence grieves.

SUNT LACRIMAE RERUM

The glittering dance of brilliants must be strung
On that dark thread of sadness which is time,
No matter what bright melodies are sung.

When great symphonic combers swell and climb
Then curl and, swooping, rush towards the shore,
We hear a faint and melancholy chime.

This might come from a drowned cathedral or
Be carried on the wind from inland tower
In market-place, or church on distant moor.

Beneath the surging glory and the power
Of Beethoven or Bach, or tenderness
Of Schubert lieder's frailer sonic flower

We hear the spectral sighing of distress,
For time is music's element and we
Know murderous time can offer no redress.

Yet which of us, I wonder, were he free
To choose, would wish away the voice that sings
The keening descant of mortality

Inseparable from all that music brings
Of love, heart-piercing truth, the tears in things.

ON THE ONCOLOGY WARD

I
At Night

Well past midnight now: outside,
beyond these still curtains, heavy with implications,
their secretive corrugations,
the wind whimpers and whispers to be let in.

A single circular lamp, stunned moon,
flat on the ceiling, dilutes the dark
but cannot cancel it. The quietness
is never absolute; sleep crumples it.

The sighs and snarls of human breathing
seem no more meaningful than the wind's noise
or the far-away whispering of a nurse;
her voice is a tuneless lullaby.

At spaced intervals the figures move,
sexless in their long vague robes,
slow and soundless down the ward,
anonymous and self-absorbed.

The pale procession will last as long
as darkness lasts. They have lost
their daytime ordinariness with their identities.
They are practising at being ghosts.

II
Morning Shift

After the gaunt night, its taut sheet
of silence torn from time to time
by sudden cries and then the urgent morse

of hurrying feet, the hushed confabulations,
darkness clinging still to outer panes
behind the brooding curtains,

comes the time of neither night nor sunrise,
a brief, noiseless lacuna of exhaustion,
before the morning shift arrives,

not seen, as yet, but audible,
an awakening of starlings and sparrows,
laughter, voices, the cold scent of dew and dawn,

a distant whisper of wind in shivering leaves,
a rumour of drenched petals unfolding:
morning puts on its fresh starched uniform.